Small Matters

Poems By
April Bulmer

ISBN 978-1-55483-572-0 (trpb)

"Less is more."
— Ludwig Mies van der Rohe

fossilized tongue
mouth of mountain
stutters first words

my walking stick
pokes the great mother
her womb bleeds green

primitive doctor
black snake hangs
from his neck

bonfire speaks
language of twigs and leaves
smoke signals breathe

big sky and flat land
seam of horizon
i practise blanket stich

root cellar
bushels of apples
i climbed a tree

engagement ring
ant bears
crumb upon its back

wild horse
broken bridle
washes to shore

morning ablutions
I kneel in the river
rituals of water and soap

i wash my breasts
a white frill
around my neck

i dream i balance in the air
a bubble rises
evening prayer

sweet water and lavender
a bubble blooms
fades in the light

dry heart
wildflower fades
in the dim morning

bruised heart
my apple
in its paper bag

broken heart
fish tears
skin of the pond

empty heart
broken shoe
washes to shore

happy heart
my centaur canters
home

my heart is a poem
my body is a message in a bottle
words etched on bone

soulmate
we are joined at the hip
girdle of bone

we exchange gifts
deer horns for turtle shells
autumn nuptials

goddess hymn
she clears her old throat
and coughs

dead shih tzu
my mother wears
a jade ring

blessed virgin and her son
miracle site saskatchewan
a stalk of wheat in a tobacco can

prairie monks worship
the suffering servant
barnyard cows moan

born taurus the bull
auntie was cremated
a red cloth draped the urn

cold at the grave
damp shadows
chatter

pale ghost
white sun haunts
summer solstice

sun
an egg
boils in the heat

astrologers worship
constellations of stars
dust to dust

Acknowledgments

Front and back cover photos were purchased from dreamstime.com and were taken by Cristina Conti.

Biography

April Bulmer is a Canadian poet. She holds Master's degrees in creative writing, religion and theological studies from major universities. She also holds an Honours B.A. in mass communications and studied dance, music and art history. Much of her writing deals with women and spirituality and the divine feminine. She is also known for her unique imagery. Many of her dozen books have been shortlisted for awards, including the International Beverly Prize for Literature in London, England, the Pat Lowther Memorial Award for the best book of poetry by a Canadian woman, the Next Generation Indie Book Awards in the U.S and the Global Book Awards. She won the YWCA Women of Distinction Award in the art and culture category in Cambridge, Ontario where she lives. April's work has also been celebrated and published widely in prestigious journals, anthologies and newspapers. To contact April Bulmer email april.poet@bell.net. For

further information about her, please see:
www.aprilbulmer.com and
www.aprilbulmer.wordpress.com.

www.ingramcontent.com/pod-product-compliance
Lightning Source LLC
LaVergne TN
LVHW010017070426
835511LV00001B/17